Focus

Cameron Bradbury

Copyright © 2021 Cameron Bradbury

All rights reserved.

ISBN: 9798713988784

DEDICATION

This book is dedicated to Jason.

May your path be clear and uncluttered.

In the darkness look to your family and friends to light the way. When no one is around and you have to do it all on your own; make sure you have batteries in the torch.

Contents

ACKNOWLEDGMENTS v
HOW-TO 6
ARGUMENTS 7
MORE THAN 13
ALWAYS RIGHT 19
WORKPLACE 24
STRESSED 29
DREAM BIG 34
EMPTINESS AND BOREDOM 42
FOCUS 48
NEXT STEPS 51

ACKNOWLEDGMENTS

I sincerely wish to thank each person that I have come across as each of them helped to shape the life I have. While not every experience was a ray of sunshine or a bed of roses, it was an experience.

Over my lifetime, I have taken all those individual experiences and created the fuel to move me forward one step at a time.

This book came about as a challenge after a debate with a friend. He has been thinking about the direction he needs to take with this life and the steps needed. Trouble is, he has many ideas and many directions. All of this has left him frozen to the spot and not sure which way to go.

We talked about all the things that could and should be done, however, all of that was just talk and lacked action.

I decided the best way to help was to come up with something that I would never think to do and go and do it. Thus the idea of this book was created.

The goal was to write and have a book published. ***DONE***.

I still have unknown challenges ahead of me, some of which I will struggle with. I have faith in my ability to generate a plan and to overcome the challenges.

Dare I say, I have *FOCUS*.

HOW-TO

I am not here to tell you that your life is a mess and by flicking through a few pages you are going to find all the answers to every question you have.

I firmly believe that you already know the answer to every question you will ever ask yourself.

Like you, I have had some bumps in the road of life: -

- Failed relationships
- Lost money
- Lost friends
- Lost a job

What I never failed to do was to lose ***FOCUS***.

I did sulk, scream, moan and ask why me. When all that passed I got back to what needed to be done and the focus that needed to be applied to that situation.

WHAT I NEED FROM YOU –

This book is broken into challenges that most of us will encounter. I will guide you to discover your inner truth and by following the instructions you will move forward.

You may revisit the chapter at any time as you progress with overcoming your challenge. Each time, building on your success.

Pick a chapter that resonates with you and get started.

ARGUMENTS

We are all born perfect and over time, knowledge and information form our thoughts and options. A wise person once said, **"Butt holes and opinions, we all have one"**.

Remember that line as we go through this chapter.

I have been known from time to time to flare up and jump into an argument. It did not matter who you were, family, friend or partner. At one point I just loved to argue and I liked the part where I won.

It took me a long time to understand that I argued to win. When we argue to win the other person has to bury the toxicity, over time you can only bury so much and the day will come when they have had enough. In your world, you registered a win and everything was reset back to normal. For the other person, it was not the same. Arguing is a negative emotion and not the same as disagreeing. It is acceptable to disagree. Or, accept that two views are equally valid. It is not, the winner takes it all.

Time and failed relationships taught me that arguing just to win was incredibly stupid. Don't get me wrong, I am not some enlightened saint. I still say stupid things and put my foot in it leading to, yes, an argument.

I have a very different view of an argument these days. I certainly do not argue to win and I am happy to stop and admit I am wrong. Learning to put your ego to one side is a skill that I am unable to teach you. One way or another, you will learn it or repeat the mistakes of the past.

FOCUS

From time to time it is very normal not to be on the same page as our partner. If you have recently has a disagreement, verbal ding dong, humpy moment or whatever you label it, carry out the following: -

1) Find a silent part of the house
2) Grab something with a timer on it
3) Use the dot below and follow the instructions

4) Set a timer for two minutes and thirty-six seconds and just look at the dot, nothing but the dot
5) Do not think
6) Do not analyse
7) Do not have a conversation with yourself
8) Start the timer and at the end turn to the next page and get on with it.

Notes to self: -

Always start with *you* -

- What was your part in the argument?

- What did you contribute to resolving it?

- Were you just scoring points against the other person?

- Were you angry?

- Did you add past arguments into the mix?

- Were you being a Muppet? (It is ok to say yes at this point).

The questions above are not just YES or NO. You are not sharing the answers with anyone so be truthful with yourself and come up with detailed answers.

So, now you have a few things to think about. Some of the answers may come easier to you than others. Who knows, you may even have more questions that come to mind.

For the questions that are still unclear on you have two choices: -

1) Go back to *page 8* and carry out the exercise again
2) Go for a walk and think about it

If you went for the walk, how was it?

Put down the number of miles or steps you took _____.

This part is not needed but may help you to see how many times you have come to this point and not moved forward.

Are you clearer in your thoughts and are you ready to talk to your partner about what happened? When you get to the point of being able to say YES, go do it.

If you are returning to this point you are avoiding a question that needs to be answered or you will be forever stuck in an internal loop.

At no point did I say that this journey was going to be quick or easy. We live in an *INSTANT* world. Instant gratification, instant fix, instant noodles. To be fair instant noodles take four minutes to make so instant is a complete lie by the manufactures. Why do you think instant can be applied to your life?

Do not complicate getting to your answers and truth by adding a story or drama into your thoughts.

Just as $2 + 2 = 4$, distil your argument into a form of a statement. Remove all the drama. We are emotional creatures, I for one have been accused of this many times.

What I have learnt is to remove all the noise so that the subject at hand is in focus and that is the only thing I need to answer.

Are you ready to give it another go? Turn back to *page 8* and carry out the exercise.

I would wish you luck but that would imply that you have no control and a magic fix will come about from thin air.

You have the answers within you, go release them.

MORE THAN

Thousands of people are employed to make sure you are always aware that you do not have the right clothes, right phone, computer, make-up, hair, shoes and the list goes on and on.

This is called marketing. While I am all for something new, fresh and exciting; I also know that the shelf life for that feeling and object has a high decay rate.

Back in the day when I was at school, we had the few kids whose parents bought them the expensive jumper, trainers or skateboard. You would look at your group of friends and see that most of them if not all were in the same position as you and everything went back to normal.

On a rare occasion, when one of your friends did get one of these magical items, normally for Christmas, you were genuinely happy for them. With, a very slight tinge of envy, which you got over as they were your friend and hanging out with them was more important than anything else.

Skip forward to today and your device of choice is your worst friend. With adverts coming in everyday and social media showing you what to wear and how to look no wonder we have a big section of people that think they need **MORE**.

When is enough, enough? When is having what is in front of you good enough? The answer is *NOW*. Time for the next session.

FOCUS

1) Find a silent part of the house
2) Grab something with a timer on it
3) Use the dot below and follow the instructions

4) Set a timer for four minutes and eighteen seconds and just look at the dot, nothing but the dot
5) Do not think
6) Do not analyse
7) Do not have a conversation with yourself
8) Start the timer and at the end turn to the next page and get on with it.

Notes to self: -

- Why do you feel you need more _____?

- What will happen when you get it?

- What happened the last time you needed more _____, you got it and then what?

- Who are you trying to impress with your new thing?

- Do you feel like you are being left behind as everyone else has the new thing?

- Are you aware that you do not need the latest thing or have the most stuff?

WOW, that is a lot to think about. You may end up going over this chapter more than once. Just because you do not have all the answers right away does not mean that you have somehow failed. If you have got this far you may have found out just one thing you did not know about yourself.

What are we going to do with all this information swimming around your head?

I will give you two choices: -

3) Remove items from your life
4) Go back to *page 14* and carry out the exercise again

What remove items from my life, you must be crazy –

How much do you have in your house that you do not use? A simple way to answer this is to ask the question, when did I last use it or wear it.

A fair few of us hold on to things just because. Some of us hold on to things waiting for that perfect day to wear them. Today is that day, tomorrow you might be hit by a bus. I hope that does not happen but hopefully, it has you now thinking.

Back to the removal of items. Some of you will find this easy to do, others, well I can feel your anguish already.

Clothes, most of us have too much. We are starting here. Put some music on, grab a drink of choice, turn up the volume a bit more and let's get the party started.

Anything that does not fit, put it in the pile to go. Do not tell yourself that you will fit into it again if you go on a diet. If that item has not been worn for six months to a year it is never going to be worn again.

Does it suit you? No, out it goes. Were you having a phase? Has that phase passed? Out it goes. I think you get the idea.

If you are not happy about getting rid of the clothes, box them and leave them. Over time if you do not open the boxes you will come to see that they are not needed.

When the day comes that you are ready to get rid of them do not just throw them away.

Donate them to charity and feel positive that you have helped to make a change for the better, for you and the person that will get the wear what you have donated.

Pick a room in the house and start again. You are now on the road to being free from clutter and the circle of frustration. As a bonus, you may find that you have a bit more money in your back pocket due to the curbing of buying stuff.

The table below will help you to keep track of what you have done and what is left to do.

Chop chop.

Room to decluttered	**Date Started**	**Dated Cleared**

ALWAYS RIGHT

Time to crank up the heat and head into a relationship minefield. This goes hand in hand with the chapter on ARGUMENTS.

Relationships are complicated, that is what I have been told. Every Rom-Com has that line in it. It must be true, right!

It is very hard to have a relationship with only you. This means you have to go out into the big wide world, find someone that you can get on with, find attractive, have shared interests, did I mention get on with and make the transition from a single person into a couple.

For the purpose of this chapter, I am going to skip on to the part where you are now living together as this is where most of the issues take place.

Going back to that pesky thing called an opinion. Back in the days of being single, you had an opinion and you were correct 100% of the time as you only had yourself to please. Now you find someone in your life and they have an opinion as well. Oh dear............relationships are complicated. Or, are they!

The following is my belief and not a fact of life.

Being right all the time is exhausting, hard work and in the end, leads to at least one argument or many depending on much of an arse you choose to be.

Let's take the subject of buying a flat-screen television. You want a 75" TV your other half thinks it is too big. You want new carpets but they have different ideas of what they should look like. Which school for the kids, this list can go on forever.

From time to time the two of you will not be in sync when it comes to deciding something in your shared life.

The normal course of action is to debate it to death and possibly do nothing as you both cannot agree on whose idea is best.

Think for a moment; how important is that thing to you? It is very hard to have a topic or item that both of you are equally passionate about. In my experience, one of you will want that thing a little bit more than the other person.

A few things to ask yourself –

- How important is this to me?

- Why do I need to get my way?

- Why can't I go with the other person's choice?

- Is this worth the effort for the outcome?

- Am I driving the other person to resent me?

FOCUS

1) Find a silent part of the house
2) Grab something with a timer on it
3) Use the dot below and follow the instructions

4) Set a timer for five minutes and five seconds and just look at the dot, nothing but the dot
5) Do not think
6) Do not analyse
7) Do not have a conversation with yourself
8) Start the timer and at the end turn to the next page and get on with it.

Notes to self: -

I will give you two choices: -

1) Go forth with the knowledge that it is OK not to be right every time
2) Go back to *page 21* and carry out the exercise again each time you find yourself in this situation

You will soon discover the more you accept that you do not need to win every topic or debate about everything; life becomes easier and you become happier.

Learning to grow together on this topic will help to solidify your relationship and help both of you to focus on topics that legitimately matter with a shared and better understanding of each other.

WORKPLACE

At some point, you will have the feeling, I have put in the most effort in this place. You failed to be recognised, failed to get the pay rise you deserve or failed to get the promotion that is owed to you.

Everyone around you is getting on and getting more.

What are you using to measure your success in the workplace that allows you to have the mother of all pity parties and think that you are being overlooked?

One of my first jobs was for a global accountancy firm in my home town. I was young and keen to impress. Due to my lack of working experience, I did not know what I had to do to impress. I just got on with it and got everything done as quickly as I could. At the end of the first year, I got called into the manager's office for my annual review and payrise conversation. What I remember from that meeting all these years later is that I got a zero pay rise and the reason – "*I did not integrate well with the team*". Translated that meant, I did not talk enough.

Take a moment to wrap your head around that. I worked hard for 12 months to be told nothing about the work I had done to the best of my ability but to be called out for not talking enough to the people in the office.

Roll forward a few years and experience helped to shape me. I am now one of the most talkative people you will find in the office. I know when to put the hammer down and get the job done and I know when to stop and smell the roses.

I have guided many people over the years that wish to move ahead with their career. Every one of them failed to understand that it is not the volume of work that counts it is how it is delivered and communicated. I am not suggesting that each time you finish a task you should shout about it from the rooftop and send an email to your boss saying what a great job you did in a very short time frame.

Ask yourself these questions -

- What value do I bring to my job?

- Do I know where I want to be?

- Do I know the path I need to take?

- What will this promotion/payrise do for me?

- What is my big picture and how does this job link to that?

Most people that I have talked to on this subject want more money because they think they deserve it or feel their value has gone up since starting at the company.

For example – if you get hired to count widgets and you negotiate a salary of 10,000 rocks a year why after a year do you believe that you should be paid more?

If you can prove that you found a way to make the job more efficient or bring move value to the company then

FOCUS

you are in a good place to talk about more money. More than one person has told me they want more money because they wanted to start a family. With that logic, I should ask my boss for more money so that I can buy my dream car or house. My boss and I get on well enough but even he would think I am crazy to ask such a thing.

1) Find a silent part of the house
2) Grab something with a timer on it
3) Use the dot below and follow the instructions

4) Set a timer for five minutes and seventeen seconds and just look at the dot, nothing but the dot
5) Do not think
6) Do not analyse
7) Do not have a conversation with yourself
8) Start the timer and at the end turn to the next page and get on with it.

Notes to self: -

- Paint a picture of your future with all the detail you can?

- Write down the known high-level steps it will take to get from A to B? (It is ok not to know all the steps needed).

- Take the first step and write the smaller steps you need to take to tick that box off completely?

- Do not get distracted by others. Your goals, your path.

- Focus on now, tomorrow will never arrive. What can you do today?

I will give you two choices: -

1) Go back to *page 26* and carry out the exercise again now that you have a direction
2) Do what you have been doing and enjoy the pity party with a guest list of one

Be the change in your life. No one is going to do this for you. If you want to take a chance buy a lottery ticket.

Outside that, you are on your own but along the way, you will find people that will help you. If you are open to help and can put your ego on the shelf for a while.

STRESSED

Stress, that thing that we all have from time to time, daily, weekly or monthly. I would argue it has become part of everyday life.

In the home, it could be around deciding what is for dinner. In the workplace, it could be about finishing a task and then having to start another one. Money, health, stuff, you name it and we stress about it

I have read that stress can be good. When the brain perceives some kind of stress, it starts flooding the body with chemicals like epinephrine, norepinephrine and cortisol. How is any of that stuff good for me?

Stress can help you accomplish tasks more efficiently. It can boost memory. Stress is also a vital warning system, producing a fight-or-flight response.

In small amounts, stress can be managed and controlled. When things mount up and you have several different things that are increasing your stress brain fog kicks in. This could lead to tiredness. Put them together and you have moved into that, "lack of clarity" space.

Now you are stuck, the mind is racing, no idea what to do or how to fix it. Most of the time we tend to ignore it and push it to the back of our mind if we can.

That does not resolve your issue. Your brain has stored that pressure point for later on and when it comes around again it is now magnified. The issue is bigger, harder to overcome and you are less inclined to want to deal with it.

FOCUS

While it is impossible to remove all stress from your life you can start to control small parts that have been causing you pain. Will Rogers said, "***Boil the ocean***" when he was asked in World War 2 about how to stop U-Boats. That then evolved into "***You can't boil the ocean***".

I am sure that at one point in your working life a well-meaning manager trotted this gem out and you thought to yourself, Muppet! Hold on a moment, have I used this???

Ask yourself these questions -

- What is the thing that I am most stressed about right now?

- Do I understand the root of what is stressing me out?

- Is it stress or fear about having to do something that I do not want to do?

- Has someone in your life had this issue and what did they do to get over it?

- Can someone help me to get over this stress point?

FOCUS

The key to most problems in life is breaking them down into small pieces that you can manage. When we put all the things that stress us out into one big box that box is too heavy to lift. However if you can pick just one item, a small item to start with that lift becomes a lot easier.

1) Find a silent part of the house
2) Grab something with a timer on it
3) Use the dot below and follow the instructions

4) Set a timer for four minutes and twelve seconds and just look at the dot, nothing but the dot
5) Do not think
6) Do not analyse
7) Do not have a conversation with yourself
8) Start the timer and at the end turn to the next page and get on with it.

Notes to self: -

Now that you have thought about what is your first stress point.

I will give you two choices: -

1) Call a friend, talk about it and make the change needed to free you from that stress
2) Go back to *page 31* and carry out the exercise if you are not ready to confront that stress point

By talking to someone and sharing you are making the thing real and helping to move into an action state because you have shared that thing.

Chances are the person you talk to may have been through the same thing and will give you advice that you can use or worse case, just something that you can relate to.

My way of dealing with stress is to break it down into the smallest parts and start with that. Once I have cleared the first part I move on to the next. It is a snowball effect. A tiny snowflake does not cause the avalanche. Gather enough snowflakes and you have a snowball, build a big enough snowball and you have an avalanche.

Sometimes it is fear of even starting that holds us back and adds to the drama. We give up because it is easier than the possibility of success.

Change your viewpoint on stress. Look at it as your favourite pizza slice. One chomp at a time and the slice is soon gone and you are reaching for the next slice to devour.

DREAM BIG

We can all live a bigger life than our current one. Hey, if you are living your best life, well done, this chapter is 100% not for you.

For the rest of us who think we can aspire to more let's get on with it.

Do you know why you are at this exact place in time and space? The very simple answer is; that it is the sum of the choices you made that has given you what you have today.

As I do not know you I am unable to write about the things that you should, would and could have done to make it big.

An easy take away from this chapter is, "***should, would and could***", will be stripped from any conversation you have going forward. It just means that you found a way of not doing the thing that will have moved you forward.

When I was around fourteen years old, not knowing what I wanted from life or even how to get it, I use to proudly proclaim to everyone in my class that I would have a Ferrari by the time I was twentyone.

Flashback – The poster I had on my wall as a kid was a Ferrari 308 GTS in Rosso Red.

After all, twentyone was a massive seven years later and I would be a proper grown-up and I would have found a way and, and, and…………..

Cutting to the end of that story, twentyone came and went and the Ferrari did not arrive. I am now a lot older and the Ferrari still has not arrived.

What the hell!!! I was dreaming big and it did not happen. I need to have a word with myself.

So, what went wrong. Looking back, it was a lack of **FOCUS**. Girls, they also got in the way. I was so bad at getting a date, fear was the number one thing that stopped me but that is a different story.

Buying stuff got in the way. Not knowing about money did not help and did I mention lack of **FOCUS** also played a big part in not getting my dream car.

Experience – that thing that you cannot buy and is found out as you go along also has a big part to play in dreaming big and getting what you want.

I failed to understand the *purpose* of getting the Ferrari 308 GTS in Rosso Red. My dream was to get the car which in turn would make it look fabulous to the girls, making it easy for me to find a date. Don't judge me, I was fourteen.

A lack of purpose and understanding of why is the key to most of the stuff we aspire to not arriving.

Over my working lifetime, I have been blessed to come across four people in my various jobs that took the time to explain certain things that I put in my memory bank and coupled with the experience I gained gave me the platform to achieve everything that I set my mind to.

This has not been an overnight success story, nor has it

been an easy road to travel. It has taken time and patients and zero luck in getting to where I am now. Why do I write zero luck? Because nothing I have done is down to luck. It is down to setting a goal, understanding what needs to be done and moving in that direction, one step at a time.

I would like to take a moment to thank the four people that I believe helped shape me during my working life to become the person I am today and for all my tomorrows.

Ian. P, Brian. F, Stuart. H and Christopher. B

Two key moments stand out that will help to demonstrate a lack of understanding and the need for focus.

1) **Lack of understanding -** *Investing when you do not understand what you are investing in*

In the days of being single and looking to make easy money, I listened to the people in the office who were buying and renting houses. This was easy and they were getting rich buying 2, 3, 4 houses and renting them out. Did I follow them? No. I decided to remortgage part of my house and use that to invest in CFD's (Contract for Difference). £25,000 would allow me to leverage trades up to £100,000. The turn around in profit was in days and not months. I would have more money than I knew what to do with. That was my plan. The reality was I lost about £19,000 and in time I came to realise that I gave my money to someone to gamble with. They were not traders that knew the market and were not driven to succeed for me.

It was an expensive lesson in understanding, if you do not understand something do not get involved. I still look back and think stupid, stupid, a fool and his money is soon parted.

2) **Need for focus** – *Made redundant in the morning, our first child is born in the afternoon*

September 9th, 2004. What a day. The company I worked for like many at the time was struggling to get money in and had to cut costs. I was fine, or so I thought. I worked hard, did my bit and others were lazier than me so I was safe.

The day came and each of us was walked into an office with HR and our line manager and told our fate. I was numb when I was told, "We have to let you go….". How was this possible, why me, I am a loyal and hard worker?

I headed home to break the news to my wife. She took it very well. It also may have had something to do with the fact she was nine months pregnant and about to go into labour. We had lunch and after clearing up she told me we need to get going. Get going, where!!!! I was so wrapped up in my thoughts I failed to understand what was going on.

Later that day our first child came into the world and instead of being in that moment and enjoying the miracle of seeing a new life starting I was wrapped up in thinking about how the bills were going to be paid. Updating my CV. How long could we survive with the money we had.

I had a hundred things going through my head and the one thing that was not; being present at that moment.

That very short time when you go from not being a parent to now having to look after this tiny thing that is not able to get by without your undivided attention.

I failed to be a part of it, I was still going to be redundant the next day and I would need to focus on getting a job.

I did pick myself up, I did find a job and I now consider myself successful.

I am not going to list all the things I have and the size of my bank balance just to demonstrate that I have made it and I am in a better place.

Success is what you decide it is. It is not determined by material things.

Ask yourself these questions -

- What is that thing I am reaching for?

- Do I need it?

- What will it do for my life when I have it?

- What do I need to do to get it?

- Am I willing to do what it takes to get it?

FOCUS

1) Find a silent part of the house
2) Grab something with a timer on it
3) Use the dot below and follow the instructions

4) Set a timer for six minutes and two seconds and just look at the dot, nothing but the dot
5) Do not think
6) Do not analyse
7) Do not have a conversation with yourself
8) Start the timer and at the end turn to the next page and get on with it.

Notes to self: -

FOCUS

I will give you two choices: -

1) List out the first few steps to your goal. Do it NOW, you have left it for long enough.
2) Go back to ***page 39*** each time you have a wobble completing the step above. Rinse and repeat.

EMPTINESS AND BOREDOM

We all get to that point where things are normal, dull, boring. While this may not appear to be a serious life problem, it can have a great impact on your life.

Some of the things that creep into your thinking and then become fact are, kids need to be taken care of. I need to get the weekly shopping done. Need to decide what we are eating all week. Child one has to be here at this time child two has to be somewhere else, your partner is stuck doing something. Sometimes I wonder how we get through the day let alone a week. Ahhhh, forgot that work thing that has to be done in double time. How are you going to fit it all in?

For the majority of us this is called normal life, but how did this become normal and when did I sign up for this?

Everyone around me is headed out to restaurants, music venus, training for that half marathon. How do they have all this time? We all have 24 hours in the day, why do I have a lot less than the rest.

The good news is and this is between you and me, it is an illusion. You want to see it because you cannot see a way out of your situation. It is also a moment in time. That length of time is determined by you.

If you have kids you know when they are first born it is a full-time job of feeding, cleaning and nappy changes. That blissful day comes when they sleep through the night and you have time back, time to do everything or nothing.

Skip on a few years and the school run starts, clubs and a host of other things kick in and you are back to square one. The rut has slowly set in.

In the end, we find ourselves, at times lost. Things are normal, dull, boring. While this may not appear to be a serious life problem, it can have a great impact on your life. Hang on, is this not where we started the chapter?

How are you going to break this cycle or pattern that has consumed you without your knowledge? How are you going to escape the motions of just doing without thinking? After all, your friends have a much easier life and can do everything. I want that life, not the one I have.

If you get into something you can get out. The only thing you need to do is focus on what you want to get out of and what you want to get into.

I am not saying the boring stuff, cleaning, shopping and ironing gets left to one side. For a start you will go hungry, your clothes will start to smell and as for the ironing, I have been told you can buy non-iron stuff. That is one issue out of the way.

Use the boring times to plan and decide what has to happen versus it would be good to get that done. Unchain yourself from the feeling that you are forced to do something. You do not have to do anything. However, you do have to decide if the discomfort is needed or removable. You could quit work and that will give you about 8 – 10 hours back in the day. The flip side of that is you no longer have money coming in and you now have a new problem to deal with.

STOP – no I mean it. **STOP**!!!! Boredom and emptiness are patterns of behaviour. These are mental spirals that you get yourself into that loop back on one another.

Ask yourself these questions -

- What can I reduce to free up time?

- What can I outsource to free up time?

- What can the kids and the other half to do to free up my time?

- Why do I have to do all of it?

- What am I missing?

- What have I given up that used to excite me?

FOCUS

1) Find a silent part of the house
2) Grab something with a timer on it
3) Use the dot below and follow the instructions

4) Set a timer for four minutes and forty-two seconds and just look at the dot, nothing but the dot
5) Do not think
6) Do not analyse
7) Do not have a conversation with yourself
8) Start the timer and at the end turn to the next page and get on with it.

Notes to self: -

FOCUS

I will give you two choices: -

1) Well done, if you completed the exercise you have found some time for yourself already. Your journey has started.
2) Go back to *page 45* each time you need to figure out how to create time.

FOCUS

Well done on getting to this point. It does not matter if you carried out one or all of the exercises. The only thing that matters is that you focused on what was important to you.

On our journey through life, we start with the world encouraging us and wanting us to do everything. No one, absolutely no one wanted you to fail. Your parents were first and very excited when you walked for the first time, then you said the first word and they are overjoyed.

A few years later you start school and you find out some kids can do more than you, add up quicker, write better and you have people starting to tell you that you are wrong or no. We have all been told one bar of chocolate is enough. Another gem is, if you are hungry eat fruit. I do not want fruit, I wanted a biscuit.

Where did this, you can do anything attitude go? Who took it away?

By the time you get to your mid-teens and your dreams are starting to kick in you have friends and family tell you it is not possible and no way are you good enough to do what you stated.

That support structure you had as a baby has now been replaced with everyone telling you what is possible through their lens of experience. Inside you are screaming, I do not want that, I want my dreams.

The older you get the more you will have people tell

you what you are not capable of. The crazy part is that they all mean well when they say it to you. It has nothing to do with wanting to upset you or put you off. They are trying to protect you. At least they think they are trying to protect you.

You know just like the rest of the people in your life, roadblocks are unavoidable. It is the fear that others carry that leads them to tell you what you are not capable of.

When you share an idea that you think is fantastic and you get excited about you may find the response is a negative one. The first thing that most of us do is to start questioning if that really is a good idea.

Your last lesson is as follows: -

1) Pick a room, venue any place is good enough
2) Silence the noise around you by focusing on what you need to accomplish
3) Write it down or make a mental note of the first few steps
4) You are now ready to take on the challenge, you now have focus

I will give you one choice: -

1)   GO DO IT!!!!

Notes to self: -

NEXT STEPS

My hope is that this book has helped you to identify at least one thing or pattern that you can change to make a positive impact on your life.

If you found this book useful help others who may be showing any of the signs in the chapters by buying three copies and giving them away.

Pay it forward. Your help for that person may lead them to help someone else.

Remember, we all started life with the world wanting us to succeed. Along the way, we forgot that truth.

I want you to live a life that is rich, vibrant and free of fear.

All you have to do is to *FOCUS*.

Printed in Great Britain
by Amazon